D0929358

GRIDIRON GREATS
PRO FOOTBALL'S BEST PLAYERS

TOM BRADY

BY JOE L. MORGAN

GRIDIRON GREATS

PRO FOOTBALL'S BEST PLAYERS

AARON RODGERS

ANTONIO BROWN

DREW BREES

J.J. WATT

JULIO JONES

ROB GRONKOWSKI

RUSSELL WILSON

TOM BRADY

VON MILLER

GRIDIRON GREATS
PRO FOOTBALL'S BEST PLAYERS

TOM BRADY

BY JOE L. MORGAN

MASON CREST

Mason Crest
450 Parkway Drive, Suite D
Broomall, Pennsylvania 19008
(866) MCP-BOOK (toll-free)
www.masoncrest.com

First printing
9 8 7 6 5 4 3 2 1

ISBN (hardback) 978-1-4222-4190-5
ISBN (series) 978-1-4222-4067-0
ISBN (ebook) 978-1-4222-7618-1

Library of Congress Cataloging-in-Publication Data

Names: Morgan, Joe L., author.
Title: Tom Brady / Joe L. Morgan.
Description: Broomall, Pennsylvania : Mason Crest, an imprint of National
  Hightlights, Inc., [2018] | Series: Gridiron greats: Pro football's best
  players.
Identifiers: LCCN 2018020763 (print) | LCCN 2018024709 (ebook) | ISBN
  9781422276181 (eBook) | ISBN 9781422241905 (hardback) | ISBN 9781422240670
  (series)
Subjects: LCSH: Brady, Tom, 1977—Juvenile literature. | Quarterbacks
  (Football)—United States—Biography—Juvenile literature. | Football
  players—United States—Biography—Juvenile literature.
Classification: LCC GV939.B685 (ebook) | LCC GV939.B685 M67 2018 (print) |
  DDC 796.332092 [B]—dc23
LC record available at https://lccn.loc.gov/2018020763

NATIONAL
HIGHLIGHTS

Developed and Produced by National Highlights Inc.
Editor: Andrew Luke
Interior and cover design: Jana Rade, impact studios
Production: Michelle Luke

CONTENTS

KEY ICONS TO LOOK FOR:

Words to Understand: These words with their easy-to-understand definitions will increase the reader's understanding of the text while building vocabulary skills.

Sidebars: This boxed material within the main text allows readers to build knowledge, gain insights, explore possibilities, and broaden their perspectives by weaving together additional information to provide realistic and holistic perspectives.

Educational Videos: Readers can view videos by scanning our QR codes, providing them with additional educational content to supplement the text. Examples include news coverage, moments in history, speeches, iconic sports moments and much more!

Text-Dependent Questions: These questions send the reader back to the text for more careful attention to the evidence presented there.

Research Projects: Readers are pointed toward areas of further inquiry connected to each chapter. Suggestions are provided for projects that encourage deeper research and analysis.

Series Glossary of Key Terms: This back-of-the book glossary contains terminology used throughout this series. Words found here increase the reader's ability to read and comprehend higher-level books and articles in this field.

WORDS TO UNDERSTAND

BENCHMARK – something that serves as a standard by which others may be measured or judged

DEFICIT – the amount by which a person or team is behind in a game or contest

FRANCHISE – the right of membership in a professional sports league; a team and its operating organization having such membership

INTERCEPTIONS – statistical category credited in football when a player gains possession of an opponent's pass

NOTCHED – securing an achievement worth noting

CHAPTER 1

GREATEST MOMENTS

TOM BRADY'S NFL CAREER

Not much was expected of Tom Brady (born Thomas Edward Patrick Brady, Jr.) when the New England Patriots selected him in the 6th round of the 2000 NFL Draft with the 199th pick. Aside from a brief couple of successful years for former QB and coach Jim Harbaugh with the Indianapolis Colts, no quarterback from the University of Michigan has seen much success in the National Football League. That is until Brady stepped behind center on September 30, 2001, against the Colts, his first of many games as the Patriots' starter. Eighteen seasons later and Brady is second to none in terms of his accomplishments and the success that he has had since the 2000 draft.

Brady as the leader of the Pats has a 196–55 win-loss record; completed 63.9% of his passes; and thrown for 66,159 yards, 488 touchdowns, and 160 **interceptions**.

BRADY AND THE GREATEST QBS OF ALL TIME
[CAREER HIGHLIGHTS]

It didn't take much time for Brady to begin establishing himself as one of the all-time greats to have played the quarterback position. Here's a summary of his important statistics:

- 5,629 career passes completed for a career pass completion percentage of 63.9% (4th all-time) behind Brett Favre who completed 6,300 passes for his twenty NFL seasons with Atlanta, Green Bay, New York Jets, and Minnesota Vikings.

- 8,805 career passes attempted (4th all-time) behind Brett Favre (10,169 pass attempts), Peyton Manning (9,380 pass attempts), and Drew Brees (9,294 pass attempts) in his career.

- 66,159 career passing yards (4th all-time) behind Peyton Manning (71,940 yards), Brett Favre (71,838 yards), and Drew Brees (70,445 yards).

- 488 career passing touchdowns (T-3rd all-time with Drew Brees); Peyton Manning threw 539 touchdowns for his career and Brett Favre ranks 2nd all-time with 508 touchdowns thrown.

- 97.6% career passer rating (3rd all-time); Two active players, Aaron Rodgers (103.8%) and Russell Wilson (98.8%) have a higher career passer rating than Tom Brady.

  Brady does not appear to be slowing down anytime soon, meaning that he has the potential to lead each of the top statistical categories for QBs before the end of his time in the NFL.

BRADY'S GREATEST CAREER MOMENTS

HERE IS A LIST OF SOME OF THE CAREER FIRSTS AND GREATEST ACHIEVEMENTS OF TOM BRADY DURING HIS TIME IN THE NFL TO DATE.

FIRST CAREER TOUCHDOWN PASS

Tom Brady became New England's permanent starting quarterback in the second game of the 2001 season, after replacing injured veteran quarterback Drew Bledsoe in the opener against division rival New York Jets. It was in his fifth career game as a pro QB when Brady finally threw his first NFL touchdown against the San Diego (now Los Angeles) Chargers, in a 29–26 victory on October 14, 2001.

In his fifth game as an NFL pro and third as starting quarterback for the New England Patriots, Brady throws a 21-yard touchdown pass to WR Terry Glenn on October 14, 2001, against the San Diego Chargers.

FIRST CAREER WIN

Tom Brady became the starting quarterback for New England in the second game of the 2001 season. Facing the Indianapolis Colts, Brady showed the Patriots why giving him the job was a good decision. Brady has reinforced this over 251 career starts over eighteen seasons. For the game, Brady completed 56.5% of his passes in the start, throwing the ball for 168 yards, no touchdowns or interceptions, as he guided the Pats easily to a 44–13 victory over the Colts for his first career win.

In his first career QB start in the NFL, Brady does more than enough to earn his first win against the Indianapolis Colts on September 30, 2001.

FIRST 300-YARD PASSING GAME

The October 14, 2001, game against the San Diego Chargers marked two significant milestones for Brady. It was in that game that he notched his first career 300+-yard passing game. Brady also turned in his first multiple touchdown game, completing two touchdowns for the 29–26 win over the Chargers. For the game, Brady completed 33 passes in 54 attempts for a completion percentage of 61% and had 0 interceptions and a passing rating of 93.4%.

Highlights of Brady in his first 300-yard passing game against the San Diego Chargers on October 14, 2001. Brady threw for 364 yards in the game.

FIRST 3,000+-YARD SEASON

How do you follow your first season (2001) as the starting quarterback for an NFL franchise after winning eleven of your fifteen starts and leading your team to their first NFL Championship in club history (Super Bowl XXXVI)? By coming back the following season to post 3,764 yards on 373 completions out of 601 attempts with 28 touchdowns and a QB rating of 85.7. The 2002 season was the first time Brady passed for 3,000 yards or more in a season, a significant benchmark used to measure NFL quarterbacks. Brady has thrown for at least 3,000 or more yards in fifteen of the eighteen seasons he has played through 2017. He has also reached the 4,000-yard passing plateau in eight of his eighteen seasons.

Tom Brady completes a first quarter pass in a September 29, 2002, game against the San Diego Chargers.

FIRST PLAYOFF VICTORY

Brady's first career playoff victory came in his first full season as the starter for the New England Patriots. Brady faced the Oakland Raiders on January 19, 2002, in a divisional matchup. The Patriots were trailing the Raiders by the score of 13–10 in the 4th quarter when, on the final drive, Brady appeared to fumble the football. Upon official review, it was determined that Brady's arm was going forward, indicating a throwing motion, resulting in an incomplete pass and not fumble. Under the NFL's Tuck Rule, this ruling gave the ball back to the Patriots who tied the game with a field goal by Adam Vinatieri, who also kicked the game winning field goal in overtime.

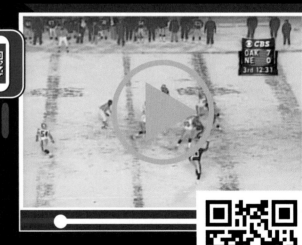

Watch Brady and the famous 4th-quarter Tuck Rule play in a divisional round playoff game against the Oakland Raiders on January 19, 2002.

FIRST SUPER BOWL VICTORY

Brady led the New England to their third Super Bowl appearance, the first since the 1996 season. In that game (Super Bowl XXXI with Drew Bledsoe as QB), the result was a 35–21 loss to the Green Bay Packers. In 2001–02, after wins over the Oakland Raiders (16–13) and the Pittsburgh Steelers (24–17), the Patriots faced a Kurt Warner-led St. Louis (now Los Angeles) Rams team in Super Bowl XXXVI. Brady completed 16 of 27 passes for 59.3 completion percentage for 145 yards and his first playoff touchdown pass. Brady did enough to lead the Patriots to a 20–17 win and earn his first Super Bowl MVP award.

Brady completes a 9-yard pass to TE Jermaine Wiggins to set up kicker Adam Vinatieri for a game winning field goal in a 20–17 victory over the St. Louis Rams in Super Bowl XXXVI on February 3, 2002.

REACHING 50,000 CAREER PASSING YARDS

Brady joined an elite, nine-quarterback club when he hit TE Rob Gronkowski for a score in an October 5, 2014, game against the Cincinnati Bengals. That catch that resulted in Brady reaching the 50,000-yard passing mark. Brady would also go on to surpass 60,000 yards passing and is on his way to challenging leader Peyton Manning (71,940 career yards passing) for the NFL record.

Brady connects with TE Rob Gronkowski on a third-and-eight play with 4:06 left in the 1st quarter on his way to reaching the 50,000-yard career passing mark in a game against the Cincinnati Bengals on October 5, 2014.

RECORD-SETTING 5TH SUPER BOWL WIN

Brady set himself apart from other great NFL quarterbacks on February 5, 2017, when he led the New England Patriots back from a 25-point, second-half deficit to defeat the Atlanta Falcons 34–28 to win Super Bowl LI. The win was the fifth time in seven attempts that Brady has won the Super Bowl, giving him the most championships as a quarterback. His seven appearances as a starter was also the most by any QB in NFL history.

Here is a compilation of Tom Brady's first five Super Bowl championships as starting quarterback for the New England Patriots, beginning with his first win over the St. Louis Rams in Super Bowl XXXVI (2001) to his victory over the Atlanta Falcons in Super Bowl LI (2017).

Tom Brady outdid himself in a performance for the ages in Super Bowl LI. Facing the Atlanta Falcons, the New England Patriots were down by a score of 21–3 at halftime. At the beginning of the 3rd quarter the Falcons went up by the score of 28–3, leaving a huge hole for the Patriots to climb out of. What appeared to be an easy victory for the Falcons turned into their worst nightmare as Tom Terrific took over in the 2nd half. He led the Patriots on scoring drives of 75 yards, 72 yards, 25 yards, 91 yards, and 75 yards, resulting in 2 passing touchdowns, 2 rushing touchdowns, and a field goal. The Patriots finished the game with a historic 34–28 overtime win, a win that also earned Tom Brady his fifth Super Bowl victory and fourth Super Bowl MVP award.

Tom Brady engineers an 8-play, 75-yard opening drive in overtime, capped off by a 2-yard touchdown run by RB James White during the Patriots comeback against the Atlanta Falcons on February 5, 2017.

RESEARCH PROJECT

Tom Brady is one of a handful of quarterbacks in the Super Bowl era (since 1966) who have won two or more Super Bowls in their career. With five Super Bowl wins, Brady has the most wins of any quarterback starting in the Super Bowl. Additionally, Brady has a record of 27–10 in the playoffs for a winning percentage of .730. Compile a list of the quarterbacks who have played in the Super Bowl with two or more victories for their career. Which of the Super Bowl quarterbacks has the best winning percentage? Also, rank in order (behind Brady) the win-loss records of the Super Bowl winning quarterbacks and their respective winning percentages.

TEXT-DEPENDENT QUESTIONS:

1. Where did Tom Brady play college football? What other quarterback from the same school found success at the NFL level?
2. In what season did Brady first throw for 3,000 yards? How many yards did he pass for in total during that season?
3. How many seasons has Brady passed for 3,000 yards? 4,000 yards?

WORDS TO UNDERSTAND

BRIGADE – a tactical and administrative military unit composed of a headquarters, one or more units of infantry or armor, and supporting units

DESCEND – to originate or come from an ancestral stock or source

INDUCTED – admitted as a member

RECRUITED – sought after to be enrolled

VARSITY – the top level of athletic competition for college and high school athletes

CHAPTER 2

THE ROAD TO THE TOP

ATHLETIC ACCOMPLISHMENTS IN HIGH SCHOOL AND COLLEGE

Tom Brady was born in San Mateo, CA, a town located in the so-called Silicon Valley, the center of the computer technology industry on the San Francisco Peninsula. Brady's family **descends** from Irish Catholics who moved to the San Francisco area from Boston just prior to the start of the American Civil War in 1861. Brady's great uncle, Colonel Michael Buckley, Jr., graduated from West Point and served in the U.S. Army during World War II. A major at the time, he was captured by General Erwin Rommell's army in Egypt while an advisor to the 5th South African **Brigade**. He was recorded as the first American prisoner of war and was eventually released in May of 1942.

Brady's parents are Gaylynn Patricia and Thomas Brady, Sr. He is the youngest child and only son and grew up with three older siblings. His sisters are Nancy, Julie, and Maureen. Brady's sisters were just as athletic as he is; his sister Maureen was a standout softball pitcher at Hillsdale High School in San Mateo, CA, compiling a 111–10 record. Pitching 29 no-hitters and 14 perfect games, Maureen Brady was **inducted** into the San Mateo County Hall of Fame in 1999, four years ahead of her younger brother Tom. Maureen received a scholarship to Fresno State University to play softball.

Sister Julie played soccer at St. Mary's College of California (Moraga, CA) as a walk-on and is married to former Boston Red Sox first/third baseman and 2007 World Series Champion Kevin Youkilis. His other sister Nancy was also a first-rate softball player **recruited** by the University of California, before choosing another career path, receiving her Master of Public Health from Boston University.

HIGH SCHOOL

Brady played football, basketball, and baseball for Junipero Serra High School. He began play at quarterback on the junior **varsity** (JV) squad, eventually starting on the JV team and moving to the varsity level in his junior and senior years.

Brady was also a standout baseball player while attending high school. He was a highly sought-after prospect as a catcher who could also hit from both sides of the plate. He was drafted by the Montreal Expos (now the Washington Nationals) in the 18th round of the 1995 MLB Draft. Although the scouts thought very highly of his skill and potential and offered him money to sign, Brady ultimately decided to stick with his first love of football and continued pursuing his passion in that sport instead.

In his senior year as quarterback for the Padres, Brady received All-State and All-Far West honors. He finished his high school career with 3,702 passing yards and he also tossed 31 touchdowns.

Watch an interview with Tom Brady's oldest sister Maureen and KGET-TV (Bakersfield, CA) and Sports Director Lina Washington from 2016, discussing the family's love of sports and how it was growing up competing.

COLLEGE

Brady considered offers from five schools to play collegiate football. These included University of California, Berkeley; University of California, Los Angeles; University of Southern California; University of Illinois; and the University of Michigan. Tom Brady, Sr. hoped his son would choose to stay in state and play at nearby University of California at Berkeley (Cal). Brady silently committed to play for the Golden Bears but ultimately chose to go to Ann Arbor to play for the University of Michigan Wolverines of the Big Ten Conference.

Brady did not come to college as the starting quarterback, instead spending the first two years of his time in Ann Arbor as a backup to Brian Griese, a soon-to-be NFL QB who had a decent career for the Denver Broncos and is son of the Hall

Brady played college football at the University of Michigan.

of Fame Super Bowl-winning quarterback Bob Griese. By his sophomore year in 1997, Brady watched as Griese led the Wolverines to a perfect season and a Rose Bowl victory, sharing National Championship honors with University of Nebraska Cornhuskers (Nebraska was a member of the Big 12 Conference and joined the Big Ten, alongside Michigan, in 2011).

Entering his junior year, Brady considered transferring to his hometown school—Cal. After choosing to stay at Michigan (where he received Academic All-Big Ten honors that season), head coach Lloyd Carr platooned Brady with Drew Henson for most of his final two seasons. Brady typically started the game and Henson would finish the second half. This arrangement created some frustration for Brady who ultimately won the job outright and began to separate himself as a potential NFL prospect.

For his career as quarterback for the University of Michigan, Brady finished with a win-loss record of 20–5. His significant wins included a 1999 Citrus Bowl win over the University of Arkansas by the score of 45–31, wins over Notre Dame and conference powerhouses University of Wisconsin and Penn State University, and a win over the University of Alabama in the 2000 Orange Bowl. His flair for dramatic, come-from-behind wins earned him the nickname "Comeback Kid" in college. Brady, who graduated with a 3.3 GPA and

Brady was drafted by New England in the 6th round at the 2000 NFL Draft.

a degree in General Studies, finished his career with the University of Michigan with the following statistics, earning Big Ten Conference Honorable Mention honors in both his junior and senior years:

Season	Completions	Attempts	Comp%	Yards	TDs	INTs
1996	3	5	60.0	26	0	1
1997	12	15	80.0	103	0	0
1998	200	323	61.9	2,427	14	10
1999	180	295	61.0	2,217	16	6
TOTALS	395	638	61.9	4,773	30	17

NFL DRAFT DAY 2000

After leading the Wolverines to a 35–34 overtime bowl victory over Alabama in 2000, Brady became eligible to enter the 2000 NFL Draft. He participated in the 2000 NFL Scouting Combine, where he posted the following results:

Measurements (height, weight): 6 feet 4 inches (1.93m), 211 lb. (95.7 kg)

- 40-yard dash: 5.24 seconds
- 3-cone: 7.20 seconds
- Vertical jump: 24.5 inches (0.62 m)
- Broad jump: 8 feet 3 inches 9 (2.51 m)

On the Wonderlic test used to assess player intelligence, Brady scored a 33, which is considered an exceptional score and well over the average score of 26 for quarterbacks.

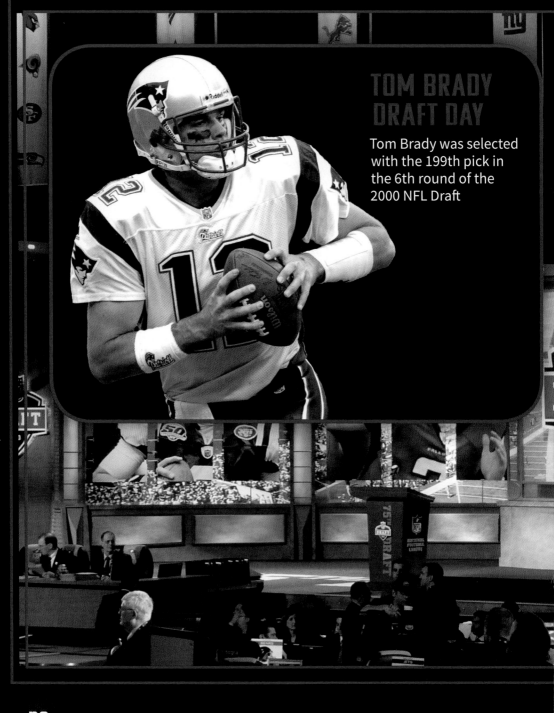

TOM BRADY DRAFT DAY

Tom Brady was selected with the 199th pick in the 6th round of the 2000 NFL Draft

The 2000 NFL draft, which was held at the Theater of Madison Square Garden located in New York City between April 15–16, 2000.

- A total of 254 players were chosen in seven rounds.

- DE Courtney Brown of Penn State University was the 1st overall draft selection, made by the Cleveland Browns. Nittany Lion teammate LB LaVar Arrington was picked by Washington with the 2nd overall pick. It was the first time in draft history that two players from Pen State were selected with the top two overall picks.

- Safety Mike Green of Northwestern State University was the last pick in the draft by the Chicago Bears, making him "Mr. Irrelevant." He played nine seasons in the NFL with Chicago, Washington, and Seattle before retiring in 2008.

- Chad Pennington was the first quarterback selected in the draft, going in the 1st round to the New York Jets with the 17th pick.

- Brady was the seventh quarterback drafted in the 2000 NFL Draft.

- Brady was one of eleven quarterbacks in total drafted in the 2000 NFL Draft.

- Of the eleven quarterbacks selected, only Brady is still active in the NFL (2017)

THE SIX QUARTERBACKS SELECTED AHEAD OF BRADY IN THE 2000 NFL DRAFT

A total of 198 players were selected ahead of Tom Brady in the 2000 NFL Draft. The New England Patriots chose Brady with the 199th pick in the 6th round, remarkably behind three placekickers—Sebastian Janikowski (Oakland Raiders, 1st round, 17th overall pick), Neil Rackers (Cincinnati Bengals, 6th round, 169th overall pick), and Paul Edinger (Chicago Bears, 6th round, 174th pick). Janikowski and Rackers both have Pro Bowl appearances on their record and all three rank in the top 100 for field goals made in a career. Their selections appear to be far more justifiable than that of the six quarterbacks who were chosen ahead of Brady.

Chad Pennington (New York Jets, 1st round, 18th overall pick), Giovanni Carmazzi (San Francisco 49ers, 3rd round, 65th overall pick), Chris Redman (Baltimore Ravens, 3rd round, 75th overall pick), Tee Martin (Pittsburgh Steelers, 5th round, 163rd overall pick), Marc Bulger (New Orleans Saints, 6th round, 168th overall pick), and Spergon Wynn (Cleveland Browns, 6th round, 183rd overall pick) were all chosen ahead of Brady as QBs in the 2000 draft. How good were these players compared to Brady? Here are their stats (not one is playing the NFL as of 2017):

NAME	YEARS	TEAM(S)	GAMES	YARDS	COMP%	TDS	INTs
C. Pennington	2000–2010 (11)	2 teams	89	17,823	66.0	102	64
G. Carmazzi	2000–2000 (1)	1 team	0	0	0	0	0
C. Redman	2000–2011 (12)	2 teams	31	3,179	57.2	21	14
T. Martin	2000–2003 (4)	2 teams	3	69	37.5	0	1
M. Bulger	2000–2009 (10)	1 team	96	22,814	62.1	122	93
S. Wynn	2000–2001 (2)	2 teams	10	585	46.0	1	17
TOTAL			229	44,470	62.8	246	189

Brady's score of 33 on the Wonderlic test prior to the draft was well above the average score for QBs.

On February 4th, 2018, Brady played in Super Bowl LII, his eighth Super Bowl. This was a rematch of Super Bowl XXXIX from 2005 when New England also played Philadelphia. In that game, Brady and New England claimed their third title. In the 2018 game, however, the Eagles avenged the loss. Brady had his best Super Bowl ever, throwing for 505 yards and 3 TDs. It was not enough, as the Patriots defense had an awful game, giving up 538 yards in the 41–33 loss.

It should be noted that the six combined have played in a total of 229 games to Brady's 251 starts, thrown for 44,470 yards to Brady's 66,159, 246 touchdowns which are about half the total for Brady's career, and 19 more interceptions than Brady has thrown—189 for the group of six versus Brady's career 160 interceptions. Marc Bulger is the only other QB aside from Brady who has been selected to the Pro Bowl team (twice against Brady's thirteen selections) and Chris Redman is the only one to have seen the Super Bowl as a player (he did not play in Baltimore's 2001 Super Bowl XXXV win over the New York Giants). Brady has appeared in eight Super Bowls with a record of 5–3.

Drafting players and assessing future potential is not an easy task, as any NFL player personnel director and general manager may tell you. It is certainly difficult to know which players drafted are going to become legendary, like Brady, and which will turn out to be busts, like Giovanni Carmazzi who never took a snap as quarterback in his

Oakland kicker Sebastian Janikowski, who unlike Brady was drafted in the 1st round, is the only player besides Brady from the 2000 NFL Draft that played in the league in 2017.

one season in San Francisco but was selected 134 places ahead of Brady. It is probably safe to assume that the thirty-one teams that chose not to draft Brady probably wish they could have a do-over, if a crystal ball were available for them to see what they would miss out on.

Brady has played more career games than the other six QBs in his draft class combined.

RESEARCH PROJECT

Tom Brady was selected 199th overall in the 2000 NFL Draft, a draft that produced one of the smallest classes of quarterbacks since 1955 (2015 produced the lowest with only six selections). He is a rarity in that very few, if any, quarterbacks selected after rounds 1–3 have proven to be successful in the league, but there are exceptions. Looking at the NFL draft over the past twenty-five years (1992–2017), find five quarterbacks selected in rounds 4–7 who you believe have had great careers (not including Brady). Rank the players in terms of total wins, years played, Super Bowl appearances (including wins and losses), Pro Bowl, All-pro selections, and any MVP awards or other recognitions.

TEXT-DEPENDENT QUESTIONS:

1. How many quarterbacks were drafted in the 2000 NFL Draft ahead of Tom Brady? Of the quarterbacks drafted in front of Brady, how many of those quarterbacks are still in the NFL as of 2017?
2. How many Super Bowl appearances has Brady made in his career? How many times has Brady won the Super Bowl?
3. What was Brady's score on the Wonderlic test administered prior to the NFL draft? How did his score compare to the average score for quarterbacks?

WORDS TO UNDERSTAND

CREDIBILITY – the quality or power of inspiring belief

FEAT – an act or product of skill, endurance, or ingenuity

HONORABLE MENTION – a distinction conferred (as in a contest or exhibition) on works or persons of exceptional merit but not deserving of top honors

REMARKABLY – in a manner worthy of being or likely to be noticed especially as being uncommon or extraordinary

CHAPTER 3

ON THE FIELD

BEING "TOM TERRIFIC"

Among his many nicknames, Tom Brady has most often been called Tom Terrific. A look at the numbers that he has put up over his **remarkably** long NFL career certainly lend **credibility** to the argument that he has been nothing but terrific for the New England Patriots. A look at the different career milestones that Tom Brady has reached shows just how terrific he has been and how he ranks among the legendary quarterbacks in the history of the league.

With his high level of record-setting play over eighteen seasons, Brady has lived up to the nickname "Tom Terrific."

GRIDIRON GREATS

TOM BRADY
NEW ENGLAND PATRIOTS

QUARTERBACK

TOM BRADY

Date of birth: August 3, 1977
Height: 6 feet, 4 inches (1.93 m), Weight: Approx. 225 lbs (102 kg)
Drafted in the 6th round in 2000 (199th pick overall) by the New England Patriots
College: University of Michigan

CAREER

GAMES	COMPLETIONS	ATTEMPTS	COMP%	YARDS	TDS	INTERCEPTS
253	5,629	8,805	63.9	66,159	488	160

- Five-time Super Bowl champion
- Led NFL in passing yards three times (2005, 2007, 2017)
- Led NFL in touchdowns four times (2002, 2007, 2010, 2015)
- Led NFL in quarterback rating twice (2007, 2010)
- Named to thirteen Pro Bowls (2001, 2004, 2005, 2007, 2009, 2010, 2011, 2012, 2013, 2014, 2015, 2016, 2017)
- Named first team All-Pro four times (2007, 2010, 2016, 2017)
- Named second team All-Pro twice (2005, 2015)
- Named Super Bowl MVP four times (2001, 2003, 2014, 2016)
- Named NFL Bert Bell Award Player of the Year in 2007
- Named NFL Associated Press MVP three times (2007, 2010, 2017)

QUARTERBACK

TOM BRADY'S NFL ACCOMPLISHMENTS

Brady has completed eighteen seasons in the NFL. During his career, he has shattered or approached many of the league's QB records and has received numerous honors, awards, and recognitions. It is not hard to imagine that when Brady decides to retire, many of his accomplishments will be out of the reach of those players who come after him and attempt to play quarterback at the same consistently high level that he did.

Here are some of the accomplishments and highlights from Tom Brady's eighteen-year career in the NFL:

- Five-time Super Bowl champion
- Four-time Super Bowl MVP
- Three-time NFL MVP
- 13 Pro Bowl appearances
- 2007 Bert Bell Award winner

Brady won his third of four Super Bowl MVP awards in New England's Super Bowl XLIX victory over the Seattle Seahawks in Phoenix.

- Named NFL Associated Press Offensive Player of the Year twice (2007, 2010)

- Member of the NFL Hall of Fame All-2000s 1st Team

- Member of the 1997 NCAA co-National Champion Michigan Wolverine team

- Selected as **Honorable Mention**, All-Big Ten Conference (1998, 1999)

- Member of the San Mateo County Hall of Fame, 2003

- Selected All-State, 1995

- Selected All-Far West, 1995

- Drafted in the 18th round of the 1995 MLB Draft by the Montreal Expos

- Played high school football, basketball, and baseball at Junipero Serra High School (San Mateo, CA) [Padres], 1992–1995

Additionally, Brady holds thirty individual NFL records for the regular season, playoffs, and the Super Bowl. Some of his records include most playoff starts in the history of the NFL (37), most consecutive playoff wins (10), most playoff passing yards (10,226), and most regular season games won by a quarterback (196).

TOM BRADY CAREER PASSING MILESTONES

PASSING YARDS IN A CAREER:

MILESTONE	DATE	OPPONENT	OUTCOME	SCORE
10,000 yards	December 20, 2003	New York Jets	W	21–16
20,000 yards	November 12, 2006	New York Jets	L	14–17
30,000 yards	December 16, 2009	Miami Dolphins	L	21–22
40,000 yards	September 9, 2012	Tennessee Titans	W	34–13
50,000 yards	October 5, 2014	Cincinnati Bengals	W	43–17
60,000 yards	November 27, 2016	New York Jets	W	22–17

Only five quarterbacks in the history of the National Football League have thrown for at least 60,000 yards in their career, including Brady. His 66,159 yards passing and average of 3,891 yards per season rank him number four behind Drew Brees of the New Orleans Saints (70,445), Hall of Fame quarterback Brett Favre (Atlanta Falcons, Green Bay Packers, New York Jets, Minnesota Vikings) who passed for 71,838 yards, and Peyton Manning (Indianapolis Colts, Denver Broncos) who finished his career with 71,940 yards. Hall of Famer Dan Marino is the fifth member of the club, with 61,361 yards while a member of the Miami Dolphins.

This chart illustrates just how remarkable an accomplishment throwing for more than 60,000 yards is for an NFL quarterback. Only 187 players at the position in the league's history have passed for at least 10,000 yards; that number drops to 107 who have thrown for 20,000 yards, and again to forty-five that have made at least 30,000 yards, notably Aaron Rodgers of the Green Bay Packers with 38,502.

Brady is one of only five QBs in the history of the NFL to throw for more than 60,000 yards.

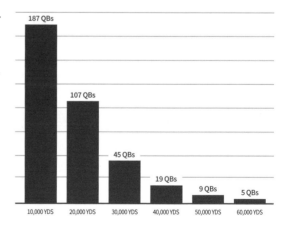

187 QBs					
	107 QBs				
		45 QBs			
			19 QBs		
				9 QBs	5 QBs
10,000 YDS	20,000 YDS	30,000 YDS	40,000 YDS	50,000 YDS	60,000 YDS

Nineteen players in NFL history have passed for 40,000 or more yards, including the great Johnny Unitas of the Baltimore (Indianapolis) Colts with 40,239 and Joe Montana (San Francisco 49ers, Kansas City Chiefs) who passed for 40,551 yards while winning four Super Bowl championships. Nine have 50,000 or more yards passing (standouts include Super Bowl-winning quarterbacks Ben Roethlisberger with 51,065 yards and John Elway at 51,475 yards) and the elite five (listed above) who have 60,000 or more yards passing.

TOUCHDOWNS IN A CAREER:

MILESTONE	DATE	OPPONENT	OUTCOME	SCORE
100 TDs	September 18, 2005	Carolina Panthers	L	27–17
200 TDs	September 27, 2009	Atlanta Falcons	W	26–10
300 TDs	January 1, 2012	Buffalo Bills	W	49–21
400 TDs	September 27, 2015	Jacksonville Jaguars	W	51–17

At the end of 2017, Tom Brady had recorded a total of 488 touchdowns. That number averages to a little more than 2 touchdowns per every game he has started (236 so far) and 27 touchdowns per season. Staying on this average would mean that Tom Brady would need 26 games (about a season and a half) to break Peyton Manning's career touchdown record of 539. Brady, along with Manning, Favre, Marino, and Brees (who also has 488 touchdowns for his NFL career) are the only NFL quarterbacks to have completed 400 or more touchdowns for their careers.

PASSING YARDS IN A SEASON:

MILESTONE	NUMBER OF TIMES	SEASON
3,000 yards	6	2002, 2003, 2004, 2006, 2010, 2016
4,000 yards	8	2005, 2007, 2009, 2012, 2013, 2014, 2015, 2017
5,000 yards	1	2011

Tom Brady has passed for at least 3,000 yards a total of fifteen times out of eighteen seasons as quarterback for the New England Patriots. There are only three seasons in which he did not reach this milestone. The first was his rookie season (2000), when he played in only one game. The second was the 2001 season, in which he threw for 2,843 yards and 18 touchdowns. He also led the team to its first NFL Championship, a 20–17 victory in Super Bowl XXXVI over the St. Louis (now Los Angeles) Rams. He also did not reach 3,000 yards in the 2008 season due to injury.

His season-by-season passing totals where he threw for at least 3,000 yards or more are:

SEASON	YARDS PASSING	COMP%	TDS
2002	3,764	62.06	28
2003	3,620	60.15	23
2004	3,692	60.76	28
2005	4,110	63.02	26
2006	3,529	61.82	24
2007	4,806	68.86	50
2009	4,398	65.66	28
2010	3,900	65.85	36
2011	5,235	65.63	39
2012	4,827	62.95	34
2013	4,343	60.51	25
2014	4,109	64.09	33
2015	4,770	64.42	36
2016	3,554	67.36	28
2017	4,577	66.27	32
TOTAL	63,234	63.96	470
CAREER TOTAL	**66,159**	**63.90**	**488**

Brady is likely to throw TD pass number 500 in the 2018 season.

The 50 touchdowns Brady threw in the 2007 season are the second most ever by a quarterback in NFL history. Only Peyton Manning (Indianapolis Colts, Denver Broncos) threw more touchdowns in a season with 55 for Denver in 2013. Tom Brady and Peyton Manning are the only quarterbacks to record 50 or more touchdowns in a single season.

Tom Brady is one of only five quarterbacks in league history to pass for 5,000 yards or more in a single season. The other four are Brees (San Diego Chargers; New Orleans Saints), who accomplished this **feat** five different times; Peyton Manning, who has the most yards in a single season with 5,477 in 2013; Marino (Miami Dolphins), who was the first quarterback to reach 5,000 yards in 1984; and Matthew Stafford (Detroit Lions).

Tom Brady is on a record-setting pace to become the number one passing quarterback in NFL history. Other accomplishments of note that have placed him at the head of the class in terms of NFL quarterbacks include:

- Brady has a career quarterback rating of 97.6, which ranks him third all-time behind Aaron Rodgers (Green Bay Packers, 103.8 rating) and Russell Wilson (Seattle Seahawks, 98.8 rating).

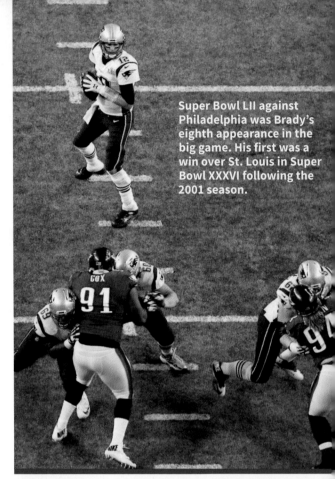

Super Bowl LII against Philadelphia was Brady's eighth appearance in the big game. His first was a win over St. Louis in Super Bowl XXXVI following the 2001 season.

- Brady has appeared in eight Super Bowls in his career, winning five (SB XXXVI, XXXVIII, XXXIX, XLIX, and LI) and losing three times (SB XLII and XLVI, both times to the New York Giants, and SB LII to Philadelphia). His five wins are the most by a quarterback, one ahead of Hall of Fame quarterbacks Joe Montana (San Francisco) and Terry Bradshaw (Pittsburgh Steelers) who have four wins each. If you count players in the pre-Super Bowl era (before 1966), Brady is tied with Bart Starr (Green Bay Packers) for most NFL Championships with five each.
- Tom Brady has the most playoff wins as a quarterback (27) of any QB; Montana (16) and Bradshaw, John Elway, and Peyton Manning (14) round out the top five in career playoff wins.

RESEARCH PROJECT

Compare and contrast Brady's eight Super Bowl appearances. How did the Patriots fare when Brady threw for 300 or more yards? What about when he threw for less? Draw a chart to show your findings.

TEXT-DEPENDENT QUESTIONS:

1. How many times has Tom Brady been selected to appear in the Pro Bowl? What years? How many times has he been selected as an All-Pro? When?

2. How many regular season games has Tom Brady won?

3. What year(s) was Tom Brady named the Associated Press Offensive Player of the Year? When? How many times was Tom Brady named league MVP? In which year(s)?

WORDS TO UNDERSTAND

COMPOSURE – a calmness or repose especially of mind, bearing, or appearance

CONFIDENCE – a feeling or consciousness of one's powers or of reliance on one's circumstances

EXUDE – to display conspicuously or abundantly

MENTORSHIP – the influence, guidance, or direction given by a trusted counselor or guide

TESTIMONY – an outward sign

CHAPTER 4

WORDS COUNT

When the time comes to address the media before or after a game, players either retreat to the comfort of traditional phrases that avoid controversy (Cliché City), or they speak their mind with refreshing candor (Quote Machine).

Here are 10 quotes from Tom Brady, compiled in part from the website 247Sports. com, with some insight as to the context of what he is talking about or referencing:

"**He will always be somebody I rely on for sound advice and mentorship. He has helped me with my own personal struggles in both athletics and in life. Greg really pushed me in a direction that I wasn't sure I could go.**"

Brady was so far down on the depth chart while at the University of Michigan that he considered transferring to the University of California at one point. An assistant athletic director at the school, Greg Harden, worked with Brady to help him reconnect with his passion and joy for the game and build the confidence he needed to not only be prepared when the Wolverine's starting job at QB became available but also to propel himself toward the next level. **Rating: Quote Machine**

"**My job is to play quarterback and I'm going to do that the best way I know how because I owe that to my teammates regardless of who is out there on the field with me.**"

Brady has a full understanding and appreciation as to what his role is as quarterback and leader of the New England Patriots. He has seen a lot of different players come and go from the team and he knows that as the one constant, his job is to do the best he can for those players on the field at that moment and time when he is playing. This is one of his stock quotes that he goes to several times each season. **Rating: Cliché City**

Brady faced Matt Ryan and the Atlanta Falcons in Super Bowl LI, where he displayed his famous 4th-quarter skills.

"I think my best asset as a player is that in the 4th quarter, with the game on the line, I have the desire to win and the feeling that our team is not going to lose."

Speaking about success, Brady shows the belief he has in his ability to lead the Patriots to victory, regardless of the circumstances. A prime example of that was his game-tying touchdown drive in the 4th quarter of Super Bowl LI against the Atlanta Falcons. At one point, he and the team were down 25 points and it did not appear they had any chance of winning. But Brady knows that by keeping his **composure** and **exuding** the **confidence** that has been his trademark characteristic, good things will happen. They did as the Patriots forced the game into overtime and came away with a 34–28 victory for his fifth Super Bowl victory. **Rating Quote: Machine**

"You want to know which ring is my favorite? The next one."

This is a great quote from Brady because it captures the essence of how he feels about competition, winning, and reaching for a goal. He is the winningest quarterback in Super Bowl history yet his attitude is to continue to drive and push for his next ring. A majority of quarterbacks in the NFL will never have the chance to win a Super Bowl championship. Hall of Fame quarterback Dan Marino is an example of a great player who only received one shot at winning and never did, while legends and fellow Hall of Famers Fran Tarkenton and Jim Kelly are other examples who had multiple chances (four apiece) at Super Bowl rings and came up short. Brady knows to make the most of every opportunity he has been given, because it could be his last. **Rating: Quote Machine**

"I'm a pretty good winner. I'm a terrible loser. And I rub it in pretty good when I win."

Tom Brady is the ultimate competitor—just take a look at his five Super Bowl rings. As a competitor who has a track record of success, he takes winning in stride, hates to lose, and has no problem reminding you just how good he is through a little "friendly" taunting. **Rating: Quote Machine**

This quote, though highly unoriginal, sums up Tom Brady's approach to the game. Football, like any other sport, is about winning and losing. He gives 100 percent effort every time he is on the field because he wants to win. In his mind, there is no such thing as playing to lose or playing to tie. This is probably why he is the winningest quarterback in NFL history with 193 wins. **Rating: Cliché City**

"If you don't play to win, don't play at all."

"I didn't come this far to only come this far, so we've still got further to go."

They say what separates a good chess player from a great one is that a good chess player analyzes the move that is in front of them; a great player analyzes the next two moves still to be played. Brady's five Super Bowl championships are a **testimony** to his desire to be the very best that has ever played. That puts him in a class of athletes like Serena Williams, Jack Nicklaus, Michael Jordan, and Wayne Gretzky. They each share with Brady the same desire to not just focus on what they have already accomplished but to keep pushing to win more.
Rating: Quote Machine

Like four-time Stanley Cup champion Wayne Gretzky, Brady has the drive to win that separates him from other elite athletes.

"We've been on the other end of this twice now and being ahead late and not being able to make the plays to win, and, this time, we made the plays to win. Just awesome. What an experience. A lot of mental toughness by our team, a lot of physical toughness. We played against a phenomenal defense and we just ultimately made enough plays. We made a couple of crappy plays—I certainly did—but we made enough plays to win."

This quote came immediately following the Patriots' victory in Super Bowl XLIX. Brady has made eight Super Bowl starts and has posted a 5–3 record. His only two losses came to the same team—the New York Giants—in Super Bowls XLII and XLVI, the first loss of which came after the Patriots perfect 16–0 2007 season. Things came together for Brady and the Pats as they were able to put together the formula to win Super Bowl XLIX 28–24 over the Seattle Seahawks and their "Legion of Boom" defensive backfield. **Rating: Quote Machine**

"I think we've got to really stay focused, and all the veteran players who have been here have got to show a lot of leadership to the younger players to help them embrace it, too, because it does get challenging and it's a long year. It's a marathon, but you can't stop, so we've just got to keep pushing along and you've got to keep pushing along and improve. That's why you separate yourself this time of year. So, we're in a decent spot, but Coach always says eight wins won't get you anything in this league and he's right. We've got to go out there and try to earn the next one."

This quote from Brady sums up his feelings on how long the NFL season is and the importance of staying focused on winning the next game. Pushing for excellence will result in success, and apparently a string of clichés when asked about it. **Rating: Cliché City**

Brady says Patriots coach Bill Belichick pushes his players to look past current successes and toward getting the next win.

"**Fate whispers to the warrior, 'You cannot withstand the storm.' The warrior whispers back, 'I am the storm.'**"

Brady placed this quote of a cliché from an unknown source on his Instagram in defiance of the NFL's investigation of the "Deflategate" incident in the 2015 playoffs, involving underinflated footballs used in the Patriots AFC Championship game win over the Indianapolis Colts (more on this will follow). **Rating: Cliché City**

TOM BRADY AND THE DEFLATEGATE CONTROVERSY

The New England Patriots won Super Bowl XLIX against the defending champions Seattle Seahawks 28–24 on February 1, 2015. This was the fourth time Brady and the Patriots had won the Super Bowl and, for the moment, they were on top of the NFL world.

This feeling lasted only momentarily however when it was revealed that the NFL was investigating a claim that eleven of the twelve footballs provided for the AFC Championship game by the New England Patriots in the game prior to the Super Bowl were below the minimum required pressure level. In other words, the balls were underinflated and may have provided an unfair advantage to Brady and the Patriots as a result, which would violate the league's competition rules.

The issued came to surface when Brady, who was 23 of 35 passing for 226 yards and 3 touchdowns, threw an interception at the 10-minute mark of the 2nd quarter from the Indianapolis Colt's 26-yard line. The ball, intended for TE Rob Gronkowski, was caught by Colts linebacker D'Qwell Jackson covering on the play and returned seven yards to the Colt's six-yard line. Jackson kept the ball and tossed it to his sideline to be kept as a souvenir. It was from that point that it was suspected that maybe New England's footballs were not properly inflated, so at halftime they were checked and those balls that were not up to the minimum requirement were re-inflated and given to the Patriots for the start of the second half. The Patriots who were up 17–7 at this point, scored 28 more points, and won the game 45–7.

The league launched an investigation into the matter after the game, releasing its report in May of 2015. The Patriots cooperated with the investigation and learned that this was becoming an issue, despite the fact that the balls that were determined

TIMELINE OF EVENTS

The so-called Deflategate controversy, arising from the AFC Championship game on January 18, 2015, between the Patriots and the Indianapolis Colts, consumed much of the league's focus and attention from the end of the Patriots winning XLIX through the offseason and into the start of the 2015 NFL season. The NFL provides a good timeline of what was involved surrounding this controversy, the important dates, and the impact the charges and resolution had on all involved in this unfortunate series of events.

A timeline of the famous Deflategate incident from the 2014-15 NFL playoffs involving the New England Patriots and QB Tom Brady, provided by NFL.com.

Brady was suspended for the first four games of the 2016 season as the central figure in the Deflategate scandal.

underinflated during the game were fixed and did not appear to affect the Patriots at all in lopsided the 2nd half.

Brady referred to the matter as "ridiculous" and did not let it take away from his preparation for the Super Bowl. The NFL hired New York attorney Ted Wells, known for his defense of Scooter Libby, former counselor to Vice President Dick Cheney and New York Governor Eliot Spitzer. Wells was a classmate of Supreme Court Justice Clarence Thomas at Holy Cross University and were members of the school's African American student's organization. The report was released on May 6, 2015.

The key to the Wells Report was a series of text messages between Patriots locker room attendant Jim McNally and the team's equipment assistant John Jastremski, both of whom would eventually be let go by the team. This evidence linked Brady to the underinflated footballs, either directly or indirectly, and served as the basis for the recommendation that Brady be suspended by the league for four games and that the Patriots organization be fined $1 million and lose several draft picks in the 2016 and 2017 NFL drafts. Brady took the matter to court, which initially overturned his suspension on grounds that Well's relationship with the NFL was too close, but on April 25, 2016, the U.S. Court of Appeals for the Second Circuit reinstated the suspension.

Brady served the suspension at the beginning of the 2016 sea son. He led the team to an 11– 1 record for the remainder of the 2016 season, which ended in a trip to Brady's fifth Super Bowl and an overtime win against Atlanta. This run was fueled not only by Brady's usual desire to win, but also largely by his need to defend his honor and credibility.

RESEARCH PROJECT

Tom Brady is not the first player to be suspended or to be forced by the league to miss games as the result of an investigation into the violation of rules. Looking at the last ten years, find examples of three other players (or former players) who were suspended by the NFL for actions determined not in keeping with the character of the NFL. Name the player, the length of their suspension, and the impact that the suspension had on the player's career.

TEXT-DEPENDENT QUESTIONS:

1. What game did Tom Brady play in that was the subject of the Deflategate controversy? Who was the opponent?
2. What was the result of the Deflategate investigation? How did the result affect Brady's season in 2016?
3. How many Super Bowl Championships did Brady win after Deflategate?

WORDS TO UNDERSTAND

AFFILIATING – connecting with or associating with; becoming a partner with

DOCUMENTED – to create a record of (something) through writing, film, photography, etc.

ENDORSEMENT – a public or official statement of support or approval

PERSONALITY – a person of importance, prominence, renown, or notoriety

TRUSTEE – a person or organization that has been given responsibility for managing someone else's property or money

CHAPTER 5

OFF THE FIELD

HOMES SWEET HOMES

Tom Brady loves houses. He absolutely loves them. He loves houses so much that he built a sprawling 18,000-square foot mansion that he purchased in 2008 with his wife Gisele for their family (John Edward Thomas Moynihan, age 10; Benjamin, age 8; and, Vivian Lake, age 5). Paying $11.75 million for the property, Brady put in time and effort renovating the home and remaking it into a space suitable to his taste and accommodating for his family needs.

When he sold the home in 2014 to entrepreneur, hip hop star, and music mogul Dr. Dre for $40 million, he was able to use some of the proceeds to purchase his present 14,000-square foot home located just outside of Boston in suburban Brookline.

Additionally, the couple owns a 5,000-square foot apartment in New York, located in the Tribeca neighborhood. The $20 million space has all of the amenities the Brady family needs as their home away from home when visiting the city, including a children's playroom.

BRADY THE ACTOR

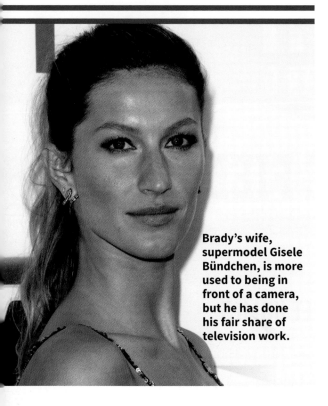

Brady's wife, supermodel Gisele Bündchen, is more used to being in front of a camera, but he has done his fair share of television work.

Brady's wife Gisele Bündchen has had her share of time in front of the camera. This makes sense since she is one of the world's top super models. The couple met in 2006 through a mutual friend. Although Brady does not have as many credits to his name as an actor as his wife does, he has contributed his voice to two animated series, *The Simpsons* and *Family Guy*, has appeared on the sketch comedy show *Saturday Night Live*, as well as in the HBO series *Entourage* (both the TV and movie versions).

GIVING BACK TO THE COMMUNITY

Brady has made the most of his celebrity and has been able to give of his time and money in support of various causes. The biggest charities that Brady provides support to include

- Best Buddies International
- Boys & Girls Clubs of America
- Entertainment Industry Foundation
- KaBOOM!

BEST BUDDIES INTERNATIONAL AND CHANGE THE WORLD FOUNDATION TRUST

Best Buddies International, an organization based in suburban Washington, D.C. (Falls Church, VA), was founded in 1989 by Anthony K. Shriver, son of Eunice Kennedy Shriver and Sargent Shriver, the man who founded the Peace Corps. His uncle was the 35th president of the United States, John F. Kennedy. His sister Maria is a well-known author and television news **personality** and the former First Lady of California. She serves as a global ambassador for Best Buddies.

The organization serves the needs of individuals who suffer from developmental disabilities. The organization also partners with another Kennedy family charity, Special Olympics (run by Anthony's brother Timothy). Through his involvement with Best Buddies, Tom Brady over the years has raised nearly $20 million since first **affiliating** with the organization in 2001.

Since 2011, a portion of the money raised through Best Buddies ($3.25 million

Brady rides a bike at an event in Hyannis, MA, in support of Best Buddies International.

Brady supports his high school alma mater, Juniper Serra in San Mateo, CA, through his Change the World Foundation trust.

through 2017) has provided support to Brady's private charitable trust known as Change the World Foundation. Brady founded Change the World Foundation Trust in 2006, and he serves as an organization **trustee**. The purpose of Change the World Foundation is to support a limited range of youth and community efforts with interests close to Brady personally. According to the foundation's most available tax filing (2014), the organization provided grants to the Patriots Foundation, his old high school Junipero Serra in San Mateo, CA, and the Dana Farber Cancer Institute.

TB12 FOUNDATION

In 2015 Brady formed his TB12 Foundation, a 501(c)(3) charitable organization. The stated mission of TB12 is to, "maximizing the health, well-being, and athletic potential of elite young American amateur athletes by providing free access to the best available post-injury rehabilitation and performance enhancement services." The organization accom-

ADDRESSING FUNDING CONCERNS FOR CHANGE THE WORLD FOUNDATION TRUST

There have been some rumblings in the charitable giving community about the way in which Change the World Foundation Trust receives funding from another charity, Best Buddies International. In 2014 alone the organization gave Brady's foundation $500,000, as reported on its tax form. There has been some question as to the appropriateness of this type of arrangement, although the money raised by Brady's private foundation (unlike a public charity) is used to provide grants for needy organizations.

In April 2017, Brady participated in a Best Buddies event, from which a *Boston Globe* newspaper photographer was banned. The organization later apologized for the incident, noting that the ban was not related to a recent negative article published by the paper about Brady's private foundation and its financial relationship to Best Buddies International.

A discussion about the banning of a Boston Globe photographer from an April 2017 charitable event sponsored by Best Buddies International.

Brady's TB12 Foundation gives disadvantaged athletes one-on-one training sessions.

plishes its mission by holding one-on-one training sessions with those promising young athletes that qualify for participation in TB12's program. The organization also holds educational events with groups of athletes displaying high potential, specifically from schools that have limited access to resources.

Since its inception, the organization has held 740 one-on-one sessions, at a value of nearly $150,000. The organization has worked with young athletes from disadvantaged backgrounds, with an average age of twenty-one. The organization is based in Foxborough, MA, home to the New England Patriots Gillette Stadium.

SUPPORTING J.J. WATT'S HURRICANE HARVEY RELIEF EFFORT

The devastation of Hurricanes Irma, Maria, and Harvey in 2017 affected lives from Puerto Rico through parts of the Caribbean to Texas and the Houston area. Houston Texan's DE J.J. Watt made an appeal via Twitter to raise money and awareness on behalf of those victims in Houston who lost their homes and possessions in the storm, Hurricane Harvey.

Through Watt's efforts on behalf of Hurricane Harvey victims, he raised an astounding $37 million, more than 180% over his initial goal of $200,000. Tom Brady, along with other celebrities from entertainment, music, and sports, gave a check to J.J. Watt's effort in the amount of $100,000.

Brady donated $100,000 to the fund created by fellow player J.J. Watt to help victims in hurricane ravaged Texas in August 2017.

MARKETING TOM BRADY

The sports management firm of Yee & Dubin, based in Los Angeles, represents Brady. The firm represents several other athletes including those playing in the NFL, PGA tour, and international athletes as well.

As a product pitchman, Tom Brady is considered to be on the lower end of the **endorsement** scale in terms of earnings. He makes approximately $7 million in endorsements annually, well below top earning endorser, tennis star Roger Federer, who made $58 million from sponsors in 2017. NBA megastar LeBron James was close behind at $55 million. International soccer star Cristiano Ronaldo, with his world-leading 277 million (and counting) social media followers, earned $35 million from sponsors in 2017 and signed a $1 billion lifetime deal with Nike in 2016. Compared to other NFL stars, fellow quarterback Drew Brees of the New Orleans Saints is listed as the 11th top earning athlete in the world at $45.3 million. Brees earnings of $14 million in endorsements is about twice that of what Brady makes.

Brady endorses a wide range of products. These include:

- Aston Martin
- Cadillac
- California Milk Processor Board
- Dunkin' Donuts
- Madden NFL 18
- The Gap
- Glaceau Smartwater
- Hershey's
- Intel
- Movado watches

- Nike
- Simmons Bedding/Beautyrest mattresses
- Sirius satellite radio
- Stetson cologne
- Tag Heuer watches
- UGG Australia
- Visa
- Wheaties

Brady, of course, makes a huge salary as an NFL QB. Although he is universally considered throughout the league to be underpaid, "an A QB who's playing for B pricing," he still makes about $14 million each season. Brady's salary and endorsement dollars, however, are a drop in the bucket compared to the other breadwinner in the household. Gisele earned $17.5 million in 2017. Although her earnings were less than the $30.5 million earned in 2016, from 2002–2016 she made nearly $400 million from endorsement deals as one of the world's top super models. The husband-and-wife team does not have problems financially because of their combined earning power.

Tom Brady's approach to competition and will to win are well known and **documented**. Where most 41-year-old professional athletes begin looking at other opportunities, such as announcing, coaching, or management, it does not appear that the competitive fire has left Brady. Whether he wins five more Super Bowl championships or runs for president of the United States, one thing is for certain—the world has rarely seen an athlete as driven and successful as Tom "Terrific" Brady.

RESEARCH PROJECT

A common way for athletes to fulfill their desire to give back to the community is through the creation of their own charities. These include organizations with a specific mission or cause, or what are known as private foundations. Foundations tend to differ from charities in that they are designed to act as a grant making organization, directing funds to different charities in order for them to carry out their work. Looking at the top five highest paid athletes in the NFL (you will need to do research to find out who they are), determine which ones have organized a charitable organization or private foundation and the types of projects they fund.

TEXT-DEPENDENT QUESTIONS:

1. Which organization did Tom Brady raise nearly $20 million for? What is the name of Brady's private charitable trust?

2. How much money did Tom Brady earn in endorsements in 2017? How much did his wife Gisele Bündchen earn in endorsements in 2017?

3. How much did Tom Brady donate to J.J. Watt's hurricane relief effort for Houston-area victims of Hurricane Harvey in 2017?

blitz – a defensive strategy in which one or more linebackers or defensive backs, in addition to the defensive line, attempt to overwhelm the quarterback's protection by attacking from unexpected locations or situations.

cornerbacks – the defenders primarily responsible for preventing the offenses wide receivers from catching passes, accomplished by remaining as close to the opponent as possible during pass routes. Cornerbacks are usually the fastest players on the defense.

defensive backs – a label applied to cornerbacks and safeties, or the secondary in general.

end zone – an area 10 yards deep at either end of the field bordered by the goal line and the boundaries.

field goal – an attempt to kick the ball through the uprights, worth three points. It is taken by a specialist called the place kicker. Distances are measured from the spot of the kick plus 10 yards for the depth of the end zone.

first down – the first play in a set of four downs, or when the offense succeeds in covering 10 yards in the four downs.

fumble – when a player loses possession of the ball before being tackled, normally by contact with an opponent. Either team may recover the ball. The ground cannot cause a fumble.

goal line – the line that divides the end zones from the rest of the field. A touchdown is awarded if the ball breaks the vertical plane of the goal line while in possession or if a receiver catches the ball in the end zone.

huddle – a gathering of the offense or defense to communicate the upcoming play decided by the coach.

interception – a pass caught by a defensive player instead of an offensive receiver. The ball may be returned in the other direction.

lateral – a pass or toss behind the originating player to a teammate as measured by the lines across the field. Although the offense may only make one forward pass per play, there is no limit to the number of laterals at any time.

line of scrimmage – an imaginary line, determined by the ball's location before each play, that extends across the field from sideline to sideline. Seven offensive players must be on the line of scrimmage, though the defense can set up in any formation. Forward passes cannot be thrown from beyond the line of scrimmage.

pass – when the ball is thrown to a receiver who is farther down the field. A team is limited to one such forward pass per play. Normally this is the duty of the quarterback, although technically any eligible receiver can pass the ball.

play action – a type of offensive play in which the quarterback pretends to hand the ball to a running back before passing the ball. The goal is to fool the secondary into weakening their pass coverage.

play clock – visible behind the end zone at either end of the stadium. Once a play is concluded, the offense has 40 seconds to snap the ball for the next play. The duration is reduced to 25 seconds for game-related stoppages such as penalties. Time is kept on the play clock. If the offense does not snap the ball before the play clock elapses, they incur a 5-yard penalty for delay of game.

punt – a kick, taken by a special teams player called the punter, that surrenders possession to the opposing team. This is normally done on fourth down when the offense deems gaining a first down unlikely.

receiver – an offensive player who may legally catch a pass, almost always wide receivers, tight ends, and running backs. Only the two outermost players on either end of the line of scrimmage—even wide receivers who line up distantly from the offensive line—or the four players behind the line of scrimmage (such as running backs, another wide receiver, and the quarterback) are eligible receivers. If an offensive lineman, normally an ineligible receiver, is placed on the outside of the line of scrimmage because of an unusual formation, he is considered eligible but must indicate his eligibility to game officials before the play.

run – a type of offensive play in which the quarterback, after accepting the ball from center, either keeps it and heads upfield or gives the ball to another player, who then attempts to move ahead with the help of blocking teammates.

sack – a play in which the defense tackles the quarterback behind the line of scrimmage on a pass play.

safety – 1) the most uncommon scoring play in football. When an offensive player is tackled in his own end zone, the defensive team is awarded two points and receives the ball via a kick; 2) a defensive secondary position divided into two roles, free safety and strong safety.

snap – the action that begins each play. The center must snap the ball between his legs, usually to the quarterback, who accepts the ball while immediately behind the center or several yards farther back in a formation called the shotgun.

special teams – the personnel that take the field for the punts, kickoffs, and field goals, or a generic term for that part of the game.

tackle – 1) a term for both an offensive and defensive player. The offensive tackles line up on the outside of the line, but inside the tight end, while the defensive tackles protect the interior of their line; 2) the act of forcing a ball carrier to touch the ground with any body part other than the hand or feet. This concludes a play.

tight end – an offensive player who normally lines up on the outside of either offensive tackle. Multiple tight ends are frequently employed on running plays where the offense requires only a modest gain. Roles vary between blocking or running pass routes.

touchdown – scored when the ball breaks the vertical plane of the goal line. Worth six points and the scoring team can add a single additional point by kick or two points by converting from the 2-yard line with an offensive play.

RESOURCES

FURTHER READING

Challen, Paul. *What Does a Quarterback Do?* New York: The Rosen Publishing Group, Inc., 2015.

Cohen, Robert W. *The 50 Greatest Players in New England Patriots Football History.* Camden: Down East Books, 2015.

Crepeau, Richard C. *NFL Football: A History of America's New National Pastime.* Urbana, Chicago, and Springfield: University of Illinois Press, 2014.

Editors of Sports Illustrated. *Sports Illustrated NFL QB: The Greatest Position in Sports.* New York: Time Home Entertainment, Inc., 2014.

Feldman, Bruce. *The QB: The Making of Modern Quarterbacks.* New York: Three Rivers Press, 2014.

Holley, Michael. *Belichick and Brady: Two Men, the Patriots, and How They Revolutionized Football.* New York City: Hachette Book Group, 2016.

Price, Christopher. *New England Patriots New & Updated Edition: The Complete Illustrated History.* London: MVP Books, 2013.

Wilner, Barry and Ken Rappoport. *On the Clock: The Story of the NFL Draft.* Lanham: Taylor Trade Publishing, 2015.

INTERNET RESOURCES

http://bleacherreport.com/nfl

The official website for Bleacher Report Sport's NFL reports on each of the 32 teams.

https://www.cbssports.com/nfl/teams/page/NE/new-england-patriots

The web page for the New England Patriots provided by CBSSports.com, providing latest news and information, player profiles, scheduling, and standings.

http://www.patriots.com/

The official website for the New England Patriots football club, including history, player information, statistics, and news.

www.espn.com/

The official website of ESPN sports network.

http://www.footballdb.com/teams/nfl/new-england-patriots/history

The Football Database, a reputable news source, New England Patriots web page providing historical rosters, results, statistics, and draft information.

www.nfl.com/

The official website of the National Football League.

www.pro-football-reference.com/

The football specific resource provided by Sports Reference LLC for current and historical statistics of players, teams, scores, and leaders in the NFL, AFL, and AAFC.

https://sports.yahoo.com/nfl/

The official website of Yahoo! Sports NFL coverage, providing news, statistics, and important information about the league and the 32 teams.

INDEX

PHOTO CREDITS

Chapter 1
© Jerry Coli | Dreamstime.com
© Mbr Images | Dreamstime.com

Chapter 2
© Scott Anderson | Dreamstime.com
© Steven Pepple | Dreamstime.com
© Jerry Coli | Dreamstime.com
© Jerry Coli | Dreamstime.com
Jeffrey Beall | Wikipedia Commons
© Jerry Coli | Dreamstime.com

Chapter 3
© Jerry Coli | Dreamstime.com
© Jerry Coli | Dreamstime.com
© Danny Raustadt | Dreamstime.com
© Jerry Coli | Dreamstime.com
© Jerry Coli | Dreamstime.com
Brian Allen for Voice of America | Wikipedia
Commons

Chapter 4
© Andrei Tselichtchev | Dreamstime.com
Brian Allen for Voice of America | Wikipedia
Commons
© Jerry Coli | Dreamstime.com
© Jerry Coli | Dreamstime.com
Jeffrey Beall | Wikipedia Commons

Chapter 5
Arnie Papp | Flickr
© Sbukley | Dreamstime.com
© Jaguarps | Dreamstime.com
© BrokenSphere / Wikimedia Commons.
Astanhope/ Wikimedia Commons
© Gary Cooper | Dreamstime.com
© Tim Bingham | Dreamstime.com
© Photodynamx | Dreamstime.com

EDUCATIONAL VIDEO LINKS

ABOUT THE AUTHOR

Joe L. Morgan is a father, author, and an avid sports fan. He enjoys every type of professional sport, including NFL, NBA, MLB, and European club soccer. He enjoyed a brief career as a punter and a defensive back at the NCAA Division III level, and now spends much of his time watching and writing about the sports he loves.